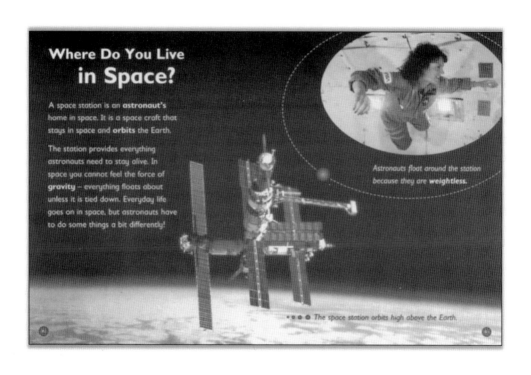

READ

Read pages 4 and 5

Purpose: to find the answer to 'What do you eat and drink in space?' and children's own question.

EXPLORE

Pause at page 5

Have you found the answer to both questions?

Speaking and Listening

Can you give an answer without reading from the text?

What interesting facts are there in the text that you didn't know before?

Living in Space can be read from beginning to end, but it may also be read by choosing headings from the list of contents. The notes take account of this.

The front cover

Read the title.

What do you know already about living in space?

The back cover

Read the blurb to find out more.

Contents

Read the list of contents.

Which headings are questions and which headings are statements?

Make up a question you would like answered from a section in the text. Use a question word like 'What', 'Why', or 'How' and add 'can', 'is', 'will' or 'might' to form the question.

Let's write the questions so that everyone can see them.

Now there should be two questions for each section, the question from the heading and one of our questions.

As you read each section, try to find out the answer to the question.

Read pages 2 and 3

Purpose: to find the answer to 'Where do you live in space?' and children's own question.

Pause at page 3

Have you found the answer to both questions?

Speaking and Listening

Can you give an answer without reading from the text?

What are the words printed in bold?

Who has used the glossary to help them understand the text?

What did you find 'orbit' meant?

What is 'gravity'?

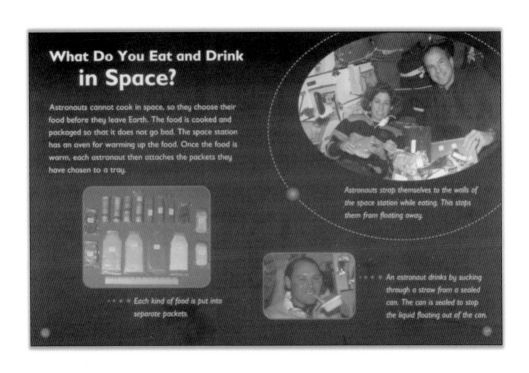

What Do You Eat and Drink
in Space?

Astronauts cannot cook in space, so they choose their food before they leave Earth. The food is cooked and packaged so that it does not go bad. The space station has an oven for warming up the food. Once the food is warm, each astronaut then attaches the packets they have chosen to a tray.

Astronauts strap themselves to the walls of the space station while eating. This stops them from floating away.

• • • • Each kind of food is put into separate packets.

• • • • An astronaut drinks by sucking through a straw from a sealed can. The can is sealed to stop the liquid floating out of the can.

READ

Read pages 6 and 7

Purpose: to find the answer to 'Where do you sleep in space?' and children's own question.

EXPLORE

Pause at page 7

Have you found the answer to both questions?

Write an answer to each question using no more than three or four words. These are your notes.

Speaking and Listening

Look at the questions again. Is there a better question we could have asked?

Sleeping
in Space

As the space station orbits the Earth, it changes from light to dark every hour and a half. Astronauts have to make their own night and day. They wear **eye masks** to block out the light so that they can sleep.

Astronauts sleep in sleeping bags. They strap themselves to the wall so that they do not float into anything while they are asleep!

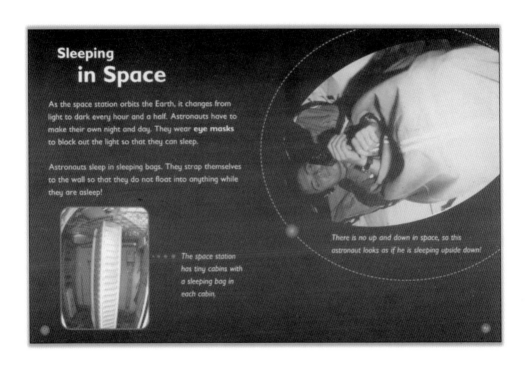

• • • • The space station has tiny cabins with a sleeping bag in each cabin.

There is no up and down in space, so this astronaut looks as if he is sleeping upside down!

READ

Read pages 8 and 9

Purpose: to find the answer to 'How do you wash in
space?' and children's own question.

EXPLORE

Pause at page 9

Have you found the answer to both questions?

Write notes for your answers.

Speaking and Listening

What have you noticed about the layout of the pages?

Where is all the information given?

Tricky word (page 8):
The word 'vacuum' may be beyond the
children's word recognition skills. Tell this word
to the children.

How Do You Wash
in Space?

Water does not flow in space – it breaks up into tiny drops that float everywhere. Therefore, astronauts have special showers and toilets. The shower cubicle is **watertight**. The astronauts dry themselves by sucking up all the water from their bodies with a small vacuum.

Space toilets use air instead of water to suck away waste. The solid waste is dried and stored until it is taken back to Earth.

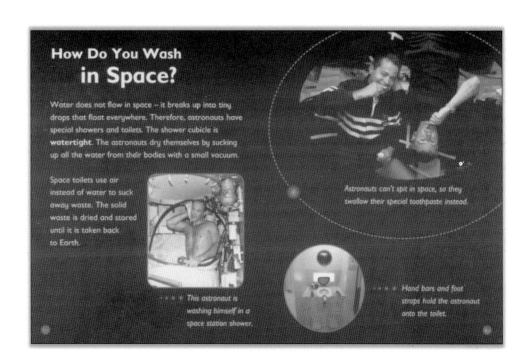

Astronauts can't spit in space, so they swallow their special toothpaste instead.

▪ ▪ ▪ ▪ This astronaut is washing himself in a space station shower.

▪ ▪ ▪ ▪ Hand bars and foot straps hold the astronaut onto the toilet.

READ

Read pages 10 and 11

Purpose: to find the answer to 'How do you exercise in space?' and children's own question.

EXPLORE

Pause at page 11

Have you found the answer to both questions?

Write notes for your answers.

Speaking and Listening

Look at the questions again. Is there a better question we could have asked?

Would you like to be an astronaut?

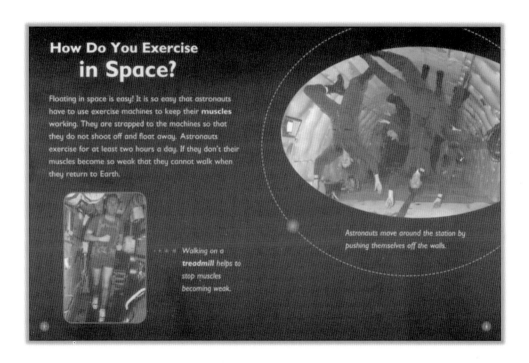

How Do You Exercise
in Space?

Floating in space is easy! It is so easy that astronauts have to use exercise machines to keep their **muscles** working. They are strapped to the machines so that they do not shoot off and float away. Astronauts exercise for at least two hours a day. If they don't their muscles become so weak that they cannot walk when they return to Earth.

Walking on a **treadmill** helps to stop muscles becoming weak.

Astronauts move around the station by pushing themselves off the walls.

READ

Read pages 12 and 13

Purpose: to find the answer to 'How do you work in space?' and children's own question.

EXPLORE

Pause at page 13

Have you found the answer to both questions?

Write notes for your answer.

Speaking and Listening

What interesting facts are there in the text that you didn't know before?

Look at the questions again. Is there a better question we could have asked?

How Do You Work
in Space?

Astronauts work hard in the space station. They do many experiments that help scientists on Earth. Some of the **experiments** prepare astronauts for longer space journeys in the future. For example, they study how their bodies cope with living in space.

Astronauts work outside the space station, too. They make repairs and they help to build new sections of the space station. They are often tied to the space station so they do not float away.

Astronauts talk by radio to **Mission Control** every day.

Experiments with plants will help future astronauts grow some of their own food.

The astronaut's **space suit** provides air and warmth. It has a **communication line** which allows the astronauts to speak to each other.

13

READ

Read pages 14 and 15

Purpose: to find the answer to 'How do you have fun in space?' and children's own question.

EXPLORE

Pause at page 15

Could the astronauts play any board games, or chess, or cards?

Having Fun
in Space

When astronauts have finished working, they relax and
have fun. Each astronaut takes DVDs into space and
sometimes all the astronauts watch films together. They
even watch television when they can get a good picture.
Sometimes astronauts just enjoy watching the stars or
looking at the Earth far below.

Astronauts spend a long time together,
so it helps if they get on well.

Astronauts still enjoy hobbies such as reading
and playing music in space.

Astronauts keep in touch
with their family and
friends by email.

Read page 16

READ

Purpose: to use a glossary.

Pause at page 16

EXPLORE

Which page was 'treadmill' on?

Scan the text to find it.

Which page was 'watertight' on?

Scan the text to find it.

Why is it so important to have things watertight?

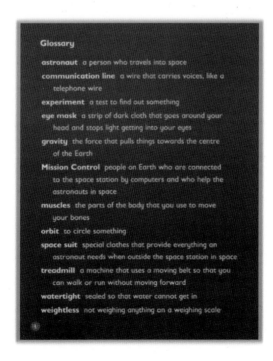

Glossary

astronaut a person who travels into space

communication line a wire that carries voices, like a telephone wire

experiment a test to find out something

eye mask a strip of dark cloth that goes around your head and stops light getting into your eyes

gravity the force that pulls things towards the centre of the Earth

Mission Control people on Earth who are connected to the space station by computers and who help the astronauts in space

muscles the parts of the body that you use to move your bones

orbit to circle something

space suit special clothes that provide everything an astronaut needs when outside the space station in space

treadmill a machine that uses a moving belt so that you can walk or run without moving forward

watertight sealed so that water cannot get in

weightless not weighing anything on a weighing scale